# "Saved from What?"...

"A provocative yet practical approach to understanding God's plan of redemption for the human race from Genesis to Revelation."

Selwyn W. Laing

xulon PRESS

*Saved from What?*
*A provocative yet practical approach to understanding God's plan of redemption for the human race from Genesis to Revelation.'*
by Selwyn W. Laing

Printed in the United States of America

ISBN 9781609578367



www.xulonpress.com

# Table of Contents

# Dedications

It has been a stupendous process that started over a year ago and now that it is concluded I would like to give a special thank you to my wife Angela for always supporting me in everything I do, and to my colleagues that consistently implored me to the finish line. I would not have been able to complete this project without the continued support and prayers of everyone involved!

# Foreword

It is my pleasure to write this foreword and to recommend reading this text. Laing has a very interesting book for people seeking a closer relationship with scripture and enhancing their personal spiritual growth. The purpose of this book is to take the reader on a journey utilizing the scriptural details about what it means to be a Christian and knowledge concerning the total born again experience to eternal salvation. The text tackles the human aspects of knowledge, truth and choice, hell and redemption, and the trials and tribulations of being saved.

Laing begins this journey with familiar topics of the fire and brimstone era of the church: God's creation, Human Choice, and the Fallen World in which we live. Every step of the way, you'll be fed scripture and foundational information to confirm your beliefs and God's truth.

Next, our minds are open to the depths of sin, redemption, and becoming born again. In this section, Laing helps you to understand the meaning, intention, and reasoning behind these terms from a biblical basis. He offers many examples of scripture which brings his explanations to life.

Laing introduces the concept of regeneration. This was an interesting section to me. I had never thought about being saved as a regenerative process. Regeneration is defined as "the state of rebirth or renewal" (dictionary.com). Laing offers that it is a continual, lifelong process. This concept was both soothing and focused upon continual spiritual growth.

Another concept Laing focuses upon is tribulation. Tribulation, another noun, defined as" grievous trouble or severe trial or suffering" (dictionary.com). Laing offers three periods of tribulation that we must go through in order to become more perfected in Christ's image and offers several accounts of tribulation by Michael, Jacob, among others.

Laing's text offers us an answer to the question of how to be saved? This question from scripture "*try to come in through the narrow door. Many, I tell you will try to enter and be unable* (Luke 13:24). Jesus also said "*the invited are many, the elect are few*" (Matthew 22:14). Laing also infers that it is not part of God's plan that even one person is lost (Matthew 18:24), for He wants all to be saved (1 Timothy 2:4). If God had his way, we would all be saved. Therefore, Laing asks that we be confident in our choice, knowledgeable in our actions, solicitous to make our call and election permanent with understanding and insight into the everlasting kingdom of which is rightly provided for us. Moreover, that we accept this as part of our faithful journey.

As I write this foreword, I have gotten into this text because Laing has provided much knowledge and insight for me to learn more. He knows that if you and I are ready to learn; we must first begin with understanding, then practice, we must do the work necessary. We are well-advised to think about these concepts and focus in upon those new to us. Read and study these examples, you will be glad you did.

I enjoyed this book and found it valuable. I think you will too! Enjoy.

Sandra R. Bryant, Ph.D.

# Preface

Most of us are familiar with the term: "being saved," but many never had any formal teachings on the dynamic of salvation and its holistic impact on our destiny. Do you have unanswered questions about salvation, redemption, justification, hell, the rapture, and the Great Tribulation? If you can't quite figure out how it all works together, then this book is for you.

If you answered yes to at least one of those questions, don't feel bad because you are not alone. Too many church leaders have not taken the time to formally present to the masses the meticulous details of what it is to be a converted Christian. Thus, many have been left with limited knowledge on the total born-again experience.

Moreover, we don't adequately grasp the significance of how catastrophic it was when Adam and Eve ate of the fruit in the Garden of Eden, or the symbolic meaning of the bride of Christ, and how it parallels the rapture according to ancient Jewish customs. This book presents explicit information and insights that many have longed to know, but perhaps were told it wasn't pertinent enough to be scheduled on any agenda…

I firmly believe that when the darkened eyes of our understanding become enlightened, then we can gain a greater freedom and appreciation for what was accomplished by Jesus Christ on the cross. Yes, salvation is a free gift from God received by faith—yet if it is a gift why are we so inept in our ability to articulate all of its meaning? Can you explain the salvation process? Have you ever stumbled in an attempt to tell someone what Jesus did for you and them on the cross? This book was inspired and designed to alleviate and simplify all the conundrums that hinder your complete illumination of the fundamental aspects of salvation.

Thus, it will allow you to become better equipped to readily explain with relevancy the truth to the blind, while challenging some of your own views, presuppositions, and beliefs about the end of days. Join me on this riveting journey as we sift through facts to discover Biblical truths from Genesis to Revelation! *"And ye shall know the truth, and the truth shall make you free"* (John 8:32, KJV).

## Chapter 1

# "In The Beginning"

> *"So God created man in his own* **image**, *in the* **image** *of God he created him; male and female he created them" (Genesis 1:27).*

God is a relational being and for this reason He decided to create a unique creature much like himself, not that he was lonely or needed to create man out of necessity, but because God *wanted* to make something that was more like himself. Thus, he would be able to have a unique and distinct relationship with this being that would be far different than any other being that he created.

Furthermore, God also decided to give his new creation authority (just like himself) over his dwelling place (earth), which he created in magnificent splendor. Man was created as a three-dimensional being—man is a spirit, possesses a soul, and lives in a physical body.

Pause right here: when God formed man according to the account in (Gen. 2:7) his material (body) was formed from the ground, which allows him to make contact with the natural world he was placed in, via his senses (taste, touch, sight, hearing, smell). However, his body could not have been quickened (made alive)—until God breathed in his nostrils the breath of life. The word used in the Hebrew is *ruach*, which means breath or wind, and the same word connotates *spirit* (Strong's Greek/ Hebrew Definitions 2004). Therefore, the immaterial (spirit) was infused into the material (flesh), which allowed man to become a living three-dimensional being.

- Through his body he perceives and makes contact with the natural realm (earth).

- Through his soul he becomes self-conscience and possesses the capacity to reason.
- Through his spirit he is able to perceive the spiritual dimension and have relationship with God.

> "God blessed them and said to them, "Be fruitful and increase in number; fill the earth and **subdue** it. **Rule** over the fish of the sea and the birds of the air and over every living creature that moves on the ground" (Gen. 1:28).

Notice, in the above passage the point of emphasis is on ruling or having *dominion.* Adam was a perfect being created to have relationship with God and dominion over the earth—understanding this concept allows us to know that God never intended anything or anyone to exert authority over us, except himself (*keep this in mind*).

Moreover, God allowed man the opportunity to choose him by giving him a command not to eat of the tree of knowledge of good and evil. Everyday Adam and Eve didn't eat of that tree signified them saying: "God we love you, we trust you, and believe your Word is true."

The Genesis account tells us that man was created in the image and likeness of God—the word likeness conveys replica, which means we were created in a fixed moral state of *righteousness (God-likeness)*. The familiar word choice that we predominantly employ to convey this phenomenon is the word *innocence*, nevertheless, they both speak about the same thing. Adam knew no sin before the fall, because of his created state of righteousness. Man was completely naked in Eden and it didn't bother them, plus they had consistent unbroken fellowship with God, due to their moral state of righteousness: "The man and his wife were both naked, and they felt no shame" *(Gen. 2:25)*.

Nevertheless, man had to past the test of obedience in the Garden of Eden. God will never try to control our capacity to choose because he wants us to willingly submit to His will and not be stoic or robotic. Our forefathers had everything they could ever want at their fingertips; imagine a place specifically sanctioned by God for his beloved creation, full of pleasure, enjoyment, and fulfillment—without fear, worry, or care. "Eden" in the Hebrew tongue means "delight," it was extremely beautiful and elegant, the perfect abode, designed intricately by a loving God as a token for his most distinguished and beloved creation.

Chapter 2

# The Gift of Choice

People who live in America have been able to exercise the freedom to choose in just about every sphere of life. We can choose our religion, career, spouses, place of residence, who we want in political office, etc. Every day we are surrounded by a plethora of decisions we have to make that will impact our daily and eternal lives. As a matter of fact, you are where you are today in life because of the decisions you have made. In other words, your life embodies the summation of all your choices thus far in life.

Yet, it's a privilege to be able to choose and make our own decisions. The reason we can choose is because we have various options or choices that vary between each other. People who live in most Muslim or Communist ruled countries are not privileged with the opportunities to make certain decisions concerning their own lives. Their options have been either severely re*stricted* or completely taken away by their government. People who live in these types of countries are oppressed because they are restricted from exercising their God given ability to choose.

Furthermore, to fully appreciate the blessing of choice, think about what if our parents, spouses, or friends vehemently forced us to love them, by taking away our option *not to love them*? We would feel violated and oppressed by them. Of course, everyone has the innate desire to love and to be loved, God made us that way, but would the volitional act of loving people be considered genuine and authentic love if we were coerced to do it? And if you were on the other side of the spectrum would you want to receive that type of love? Absolutely not, most of us desire love that is one-hundred percent volitional, and that is how we know it is bonafide.

God is the same way; he loves us so much that he allows us the freedom to choose Him. Throughout the scriptures the gift of choice is evident: "And if it seem evil unto you to serve the LORD, choose you this day whom ye will serve; whether the gods which your fathers served that were on the other side of the flood, or the gods of the Amorites, in whose land ye dwell: but as for me and my house, we will serve the Lord "(Josh. 24:15, KJV). Choosing God is always an option given, but never a mandated law.

Moreover, we must understand that having at least two different options validates our ability to choose, which means for choice to be legitimate it must have at least two options that have some type of disparity between each other (they can't be the same thing).

Adam and Eve were presented with options, which would validate their obedience. You can not truly exercise genuine obedience without an alternative choice that is somewhat different from the other. For example, if I ask you to choose what you wanted for lunch, but

I only presented you with two green apples for choices—then the only thing you could possibly choose would be a green apple. Therefore, I'm not really giving you a choice because both options are the same with no disparity. But in order for you to really have what would be constituted as a choice, the options presented to you must differ and contrast in some way. If I presented a green and red apple or apples and oranges, this would present you with a choice because even though both are the same fruit (green and red apples), but they differ in color, so there's some type of disparity. This is why God allowed both trees to be in the midst of the garden—Adam and Eve had to be given a choice.

In fact, Adam & Eve's obedience could not be proven genuine if both trees were just the tree of life—the tree of knowledge of good and evil was necessary, even down to its geographical location. Therefore, the "gift of choice" is essentially the gift that validated man's obedience, which allows his love to be authentic. God wanted free love not a love that was manipulated or coerced... This is one of the many attributes that makes God good, because he could have easily made us with no free will, but instead he loved us enough to give us "choice."

Furthermore, we have the propensity as humans to accentuate the negative rather than the positive. For example, we tend to focus more on what Adam was told "not" to eat versus what he was told he could freely eat. Adam could eat of *all* the trees except for one. Thus, he was not limited in his profusion of selections, but God only forbid one tree from him out of many, and it was mainly for his own protection. (I'll pick this point up again in the next chapter).

> *"And the LORD God commanded the man, "You are free to eat from any tree in the garden; but you must not eat from the tree of the knowledge of good and evil, for when you eat of it you will surely die"* (Gen. 2:16-17).

The above passage was the first command in the Bible with a consequence. Let me emphasize that the tree itself was not evil within itself because God created it—the tree possessed the *knowledge* of **good** and **evil—**not that it was evil. Adam and Eve only had a fixed moral condition of righteousness—they were totally oblivious to the *knowledge of evil*, as stated earlier. Satan sought diligently for an opportunity to induce Eve, and through Eve tempt Adam.

The tree of knowledge of good and evil according to scripture was in the middle or center of the garden (Gen. 3:3). Why would God have that tree in the middle of the garden, why wasn't it placed somewhere isolated in a remote place? I'll be glad to answer this question. The tree was placed in the middle of the garden to give Adam and Eve the opportunity to exercise their ability to choose. Every day they were reminded that they had choices. God delights in our obedience more than anything else, and through our obedience we demonstrate our allegiance to him.

Many people, and even some Christians, believe that by their own good works they can earn their way to heaven, but that is an erroneous belief. They misunderstand God's original plan for salvation. The truth is good works are good and we who are justified should do them. However, by no means will doing good works and being a good person ever justify us to God. Just as God demanded obedience from Adam and Eve, which approved their righteousness, it was not in any of their works, so righteousness was always and will always be established through faith and obedience.

"And if we are careful to obey all this law before the Lord our God, as he has commanded us, that will be our righteousness" (Deut. 6:25).

"But Samuel replied: "Does the Lord delight in burnt offerings and sacrifices as much as in obeying the voice of the Lord? To obey is better than sacrifice, and to heed is better than the fat of rams." (1 Sam. 15:22).

Ultimately, obedience is the key factor in choosing. We must resist the proclivity to do what is right in our own eyes and obey God's Word. The Father always knows what is best for us because He possesses foreknowledge and desires only that we prosper in His plan. "Walk in all the way that the Lord your God has commanded you, so that you may live and prosper and prolong your days in the land that you will possess" (Deut. 5:33, NIV).

## Chapter 3

# "A Fallen World"

The pervading essence of sin is that it always seeks to entice, ensnare and capture. During the enticement sin will parade itself as pleasurable, and it is, but only for a season (Heb. 11:25). The fact is if sin did not have a component of pleasure we would not be drawn to it like we are. Thus, sin will always seem attractive from a distance, but what are not revealed immediately are the consequences, brokenness, and the affliction that follows after.

It is nearly impossible for someone who is ensnared to realize it immediately. Usually the ensnared person does not realize their entrapment until it is too late, (think about how a spider works). The scriptures, however present for us some of the produce of the entrapments of sin: "At one time we too were foolish, disobedient, deceived and enslaved by all kinds of passions and **pleasure**s. We lived in malice and envy, being hated and hating one another" (Titus 3:3, NIV).

Once we have been enticed and ensnared then we become prisoners to that particular sin or bad habit. We can utilize any addiction, but let us examine a drug for example. In the initial stages he or she is in full control. They partake of the drug on a casual basis or when they want to. However, as time goes on they will find themselves addicted and dependent on that drug. They will sell their home, car, body, valuables, and steal from others just to pay for drugs. Now that sin has them in captivity, they are prisoners that have to serve their drug habit at any cost.

However, some might be saying well I am not addicted to drugs or alcohol. Okay, but my question to you is what sin has taken you captive? Is it sex, lying, stealing, cheating, over-eating, etc.? The fact is, friend, if you don't know the power of salvation you have been taken captive by at least one sin.

Sin and the sinful nature made it necessary for some type of healing and deliverance. The reason for healing is once you have been broken out of what could be years of a sinful habit you will need to be emotionally healed from the pain, suffering, and brokenness that came about as a result.

Diabolic forces are behind every addiction and every sin. Their terror on mankind is to destroy us emotionally and physically with their temptation and satanic onslaughts. Think about it for a second, how could something that was so pleasurable turn around and bite you like a snake? And the continuation of sin produces first spiritual and eventually physical death. "For the wages of sin is death, but the gift of God is eternal life in Christ Jesus our Lord" (Rom. 6:23, NIV). Thankfully, this is why Jesus came: "He who does what is sinful is of the devil, because the devil has been sinning from the beginning. The reason the Son of

God appeared was to destroy the devil's work" (1 John 3:8).

Theoretically speaking it is a great possibility that Satan understood the dynamics of what would subsequently transpire to all of creation as a result of his temporary victory over Adam. Let us examine some of these variables:

1. All of creation would be in a fallen corrupted state.
2. He would invoke the curse of death (spiritual & physical).

3. He would undermine God's authority by causing his prized creation to transgress against his law through disobedience.
4. He would receive the authority of Adam to rule over the earth or world systems, thus enabling him to become the god of this world.

Nevertheless, it doesn't matter if Satan had full, partial, or no comprehension of the above dynamics, but all of them became a consequence of what we theologically name the "Great Fall." With this single act of disobedience the entire cosmos was thrust into universal disorder. The enemy won through his inducement of Eve, convincing her that God was trying to keep them from something good (Gen. 3:4) and through her he was able to influence Adam, who watched everything go down (without trying to stop it). The first Adam chose to die with his wife, rather than to die for her.

Adam and Eve were taken down by the enemy's three weapons of mass destruction: *lust of the flesh, lust of the eyes, and pride of life*. Ironically, the enemy still utilizes these diabolic weapons today in his onslaughts of temptation.

"When the woman saw that the fruit of the tree was good for food and pleasing to the eye, and also desirable for gaining wisdom, she took some and ate it. She also gave some to her husband, who was with her, and he ate it" (Gen.3:6).

Understanding how the enemy works gives us understanding, which can lead to consistent victory. The apostle John gave us this profound truth disclosing the weapons of the enemy: "For all that is in the world, the lust of the flesh, and the lust of the eyes, and the pride of life, is not of the Father, but is of the world" (1 John 2:16). Let me break down the dynamics of the temptation in Eden and how it paralleled what took place in the garden:

I. When the woman saw that the fruit of the tree was good for food (lust of the flesh or physical desires).

II. Pleasing to the eye (lust of the eyes or personal desires).

III. Desirable for gaining wisdom (pride of Life or self interests).

On the most catastrophic day of human existence the entire creation became subjected to a curse of death. The serpent was cursed, the land was cursed, the labor of man would no longer be easy, and women would experience pain during childbirth (Gen. 3:14-19). God's perfect world now became infiltrated with corruption, chaos, and sin. To signify the temporary separation Adam and Eve were expelled from Eden and angels were sent to guard the tree of life making it inaccessible. Out of His bowels of mercy God committed the first sacrifice and clothed Adam and Eve with the skin of the animal—thus inaugurating blood sacrifice as atonement for sin.

"The Lord God made garments of skin for Adam and his wife and clothed them" (Gen.

3:21). Blood has a powerful spiritual concept that many of us don't understand. Scripture states: "In fact, the law requires that nearly everything be cleansed with blood and without the shedding of blood there is no forgiveness" (Heb. 9:22). This scripture in the New Testament is alluding to this particular scripture in the Old Testament: "For the life of a creature is in the blood, and I have given it to you to make atonement for yourselves on the altar; it is the blood that makes atonement for one's life" (Lev. 17:11). Without blood shed there can be no forgiveness by God. This is a kingdom principle and a phenomenon within itself. It is imperative to understand this concept in order to fully appreciate the gracious act of Jesus' atonement on the cross.

Also, when Adam and Eve rebelled against God it broke their perfect harmonious relationship and it allowed mankind to develop a sinful nature. This is evident when for the first time Adam and Eve quickly recognized the fact that they were naked and tried foolishly to hide themselves (Gen. 3:10). Keep in mind that they were always naked, but never knew until that point—immediately they were ashamed. Thus, allowing us to see the ripple effects of sin and how it eventually leads us to shame and embarrassment.

Wherefore, the tree of knowledge of good and evil did give Adam and Eve knowledge of unrighteousness (sin) that they never knew. Created in the explicit image of God they were only cognizant of righteousness. But with the travesty on hand their minds became open to a constant evil of iniquity without any regulation. Sin became a predominant force and Adam and Eve would soon feel the detrimental effects of a fallen world through the murder of their son Abel by their other son Cain.

In fact, mankind immediately would start to experience moral degradation on every level because of their new inherited sinful nature. Man became rambunctiously defiant against God and His laws in just a few generations. Each generation degenerated lower than the previous, which would culminate in a great destruction of epic portions known as *Great Deluge* or *Noah's Flood:* "God saw how corrupt the earth had become, for all the people on earth had corrupted their ways. So God said to Noah, I am going to put an end to all people, for the earth is filled with violence because of them. I am surely going to destroy both them and the earth" (Gen. 6:12).Yet, before the promise of great destruction, God did not leave Adam and Eve hopeless, but instead made them a certain promise of redemption with the first messianic prophecy, which would be birthed through the seed of the woman: "And I will put enmity between you and the woman, and between your offspring and hers; he will crush your head, and you will strike his heel" (Gen. 3:15).

Adam immediately responded in faith by saying: "Adam named his wife Eve, because she would become the mother of all the living" (Gen. 3:20). He understood that one day a son would come through his offspring, who would reconcile man back to God and right the ship—in affirmation of his belief he responded by naming his wife Eve. Though they never realized the manifestation of this promise during their lifetime, they certainly looked forward in hope to that day, and they taught it to their progeny and they did likewise.

Moreover, to leave Adam and Eve hopeless would have been futile, God knew that there can be no faith without hope and no hope without faith—these two are synchronized working hand-in-hand. "Now faith is being sure of what we hope for and certain of what we do not see" (Heb. 11:1). Faith both believes for present realities and future expectations (hope). Subsequently, mankind has always been anticipating the coming of the Messiah, the man who would be like Adam before the fall and reconcile creation back to the Creator. That is why the Paul calls Christ the last Adam.

## Chapter 4

# Hell

The subject of hell has been at the epicenter of an exponential amount of debates around the world. The topic in itself is highly complex and it is expressed on two different extremes and neither one are appropriate for dealing with such a destructive place. (1) It has been pontificated as a means of coercion and manipulation by many evangelicals to vehemently compel those that are non-Christians to become Christians or (2) It has been completely ignored as irrelevant and treated as *taboo.* Consequently, many people have many misconceptions and some have a dubious understanding on this subject. Many perplexing emotions and a variety of questions arise in the hearts of the masses. It has even been the causal agent for many Christians to turn away from the truth of God's word. What is hell, who goes there and why, where is it located, and why would a loving God send people to such a horrific place?

To tackle this colossal of a subject we must perceive God's actions throughout the Bible. For example, God is good and because He is good he must punish evil and evil doers. For instance, take our judicial system here in America—does it not punish crime and those that do them (criminals)? Do we ever say that our judicial system is evil within itself? What if criminals were able to readily commit crimes without any type of punishment or consequences? The answer is we would have total dismay, corruption, and violence of every nature. People would be afraid to leave their homes or better yet stay in their homes; no one would be safe at any place at any time (to say the least), we would have total anarchy.

However, God's judicial system is far greater than ours because His judgments are thoroughly righteous. Our judicial system does not always make the right decisions, because imperfect humans run it, but the system in itself is absolutely necessary for all of us to co-exist in a peaceable order. God's righteous judgment can be traced throughout the New Testament from Adam and Eve's banishment from Eden, Noah's epic flood, the destruction of Sodom and Gomorrah, to the final judgment in the book of Revelation. We must conceive within our minds that God has the right to judge the world by whatever premise He chooses on the basis of being the Creator. You will always be able to judge that which you have ownership over.

Hell is defined as: a place of eternal punishment; the abode of condemned souls and devils; a state of eternal separation from God. (Nelson's Bible Dictionary, 2004) There are four main distinctive terms used in the Bible when speaking of hell

1. **She'ol** (Heb. Strong's Greek/Hebrew Definitions, 2004) means the state of

death: a place of conscious existence after death.

2. **Hades** (Grk.) - properly, unseen, "Hades" or the place (state) of departed souls.

3. **Tartaroo (Grk) -** the name for the subterranean region, where you suffer punishment for evil deeds, it is referenced in the following scripture: "For if God did not spare angels when they sinned, but sent them to hell, putting them into gloomy dungeons to be held for judgment…" (2 Pet. 2:4, NIV).

4. **Gehenna**- the valley of Hinnom. A place where the Jewish apostasies, the rites of Molech, were celebrated (1 Kings 11:7). King Josiah converted it into a place of abomination, where dead bodies were thrown and burned (2 Kings 23:13-14). Hence the place served as a symbol, and the name was appropriated to designate the abode of lost spirits.

In this particular story in the NT Jesus vividly spoke about hell and what it is comprised of: "There was a rich man who was dressed in purple and fine linen and lived in luxury every day. At his gate was laid a beggar named Lazarus, covered with sores and longing to eat what fell from the rich man's table. Even the dogs came and licked his sores."(Luke 16:19-10, NIV)

- This story compares and contrasts the disparity of the eternal state of the poor beggar and a rich man.

The time came when the beggar died and the angels carried him to **Abraham's side**. The rich man also died and was buried. **In hell, where he was in torment**, he looked up and saw Abraham far away, with Lazarus by his side. So he called to him, Father Abraham, have pity on me and send Lazarus to dip the tip of his finger in water and cool my tongue, because I am in agony in this fire (Luke 16:22-24, NIV)

- Both men died, one is carried into Abraham's side (temporal heaven).

"But Abraham replied, 'Son, remember that in your lifetime you received your good things, while Lazarus received bad things, but now he is comforted here and you are in agony. And besides all this, between us and you a great chasm has been fixed, so that those who want to go from here to you cannot, nor can anyone cross over from there to us" (Luke 16:25-26).

- Afflicted with tormenting pain and fire.
- We can deduce that the rich man lived a sensual and sinful lifestyle, while Lazarus was a righteous and humble man.
- Lazarus doesn't experience any agony or pain, which is the opposite from the rich man.
- There is a rift between the places, which disannuls the ability to escape from hell.

"He answered, Then I beg you, father, send Lazarus to my father's house, for I have five brothers. Let him warn them, so that they will not also come to this place of torment.

Abraham replied, they have Moses and the Prophets; let them listen to them. No, father Abraham, he said, but if someone from the dead goes to them, they will repent. He said to him, If they do not listen to **Moses and the Prophets**, they will not be convinced even if someone rises from the dead" (Luke. 16:19-31).

- The rich man desires for his family to be forewarned, but Father Abraham tells the rich man that they must listen to Moses and the Prophets. The teachings of Moses and the Prophets are all recorded in the Old Testament, which is the first part of the Bible. Wherefore, the revelation is the only thing that can save people from ending up in hell for eternity is if they believe in the words written in the Bible.

Though the above scripture is in parabolic form it answers many questions about hell and the certainty thereof. There are always truths fixed in the vein of parables.

Secondly, if hell is a real place then it must have a geographical location. The scriptures are very clear about the physical location as well. After Christ died on the cross he descended into hell and announced his victory on the cross: "What does he ascended mean except that he also descended to the **lower, earthly regions**? He who descended is the very one who ascended higher than all the heavens, in order to fill the whole universe" (Eph. 4:9-10, NIV).

"For as Jonah was three days and three nights in the belly of a huge fish, so the Son of Man will be three days and three nights in the **heart of the earth**" (Matt. 12:40, NIV).

The account of the rebellion of Dathan and Abiram in the Old Testament gives us a profound account of hell's location and reality: "And the earth opened her mouth, and swallowed them up, and their houses, and all the men that appertained unto Korah, and all their goods. They, and all that appertained to them, went down alive into the **pit**, and the **earth closed upon them**: and they perished from among the congregation" (Num. 16:32-33, KJV).

"The great 'pit' [hell] would only need to be about 100 miles or less in diameter to contain, with much room to spare, all the forty billion or so people who have ever lived, assuming their 'spiritual' bodies are the same size as their physical bodies"

(Henry M. Morris, *The Bible Has the Answer*, p. 220). Plus, scientists have also confirmed that the earth's inner core is hotter than the surface of the sun.

Based on the substantial amount of scriptural evidence, there can't be any speculation as to the fact that hell is real and the physical location is in the center of the earth. The fact is before Jesus' triumphant death on the cross hell was not only a holding cell for the unrighteous but the righteousness went there as well from Adam until Christ. (I know some might be shocked by this, but it's the truth).

In proof, if we go back to the earlier story of the rich man and Lazarus we find both of them in the same location, but they are separated by a great rift. Again, it's imperative to know that one suffered and was comforted. The great underground was divided into distinctive sections, one is better known as Abraham's bosom (where all those that died in faith went) and Hades (where all the unrighteous went), however this was transient for the righteous. It had to be so because Jesus had not yet paid the price for redemption, which would allow man the privilege of going into the Father's presence (the third heaven) at their appointed time of death.

Subsequently, when Christ died, being the propitiator of our sins and the reconciler between God and men, He was then able to deliver all those saints that died and take their souls to the third heaven or the place where God lives (Eph. 2:16).

It's vital to remember that hell was a place initially created by God to punish the fallen angels and Satan for their rebellion against Him—it was not originally created for mankind (Matt. 25:41, Rev. 12:9). The fact is since the fall; God has deliberated the end of all things as we know it, which has mankind and the cosmos on a collision course with eternal damnation. Everyone that does not accept the free gift of salvation will be judged like a fallen angel.

You might have heard some people utter the proverbial saying that "God's going to send you to hell." However, this is far from the truth. God does not send anyone to hell; people choose to go based on their personal rejection of Jesus Christ, which is the only ticket out (refer to chapter 1, *Gift of Choice*).

Yet, I realize the difficulty for many to conceptualize the idea that time as we know it is quickly winding down. How can this be true when our eyes have seen global proliferation of technology (internet, computers, satellite, media, etc.), plus the advances in medical science all within the last decade or so? It would seem as if we have made great strides within the human race (and we have).

Nevertheless, these things also constitute the fulfillment of scripture and they are prophetic of the end time: "But thou, O Daniel, shut up the words, and seal the book, even to the time of the end: many shall run to and fro, and knowledge shall be increased" (Dan. 12:4, KJV). These advances don't tell the real story of where we are as a people. Although we had all of these significant advances—collectively mankind has plummeted into great depths of moral depravity and the law of sin and death has had a degenerative impact in the world.

The seas are raging, volcanoes are erupting, earthquakes, tornadoes and hurricanes are bolstering in various places (Matt. 24:7). These are all signs indicative of the end of this age. Albeit, we must fight against the proclivity of procrastination, which will cause us to delay our decision for Christ in the temporal existence of time. Some might ask why? Time is the only dimension when we possess the opportunity to choose where we spend eternity. Thus, when we pass from time to eternity via death, it will be too late to choose Christ. All choosing must be done while the individual yet exists in the dimension of time.

## Chapter 5

# Redemption

The word redeems means to purchase or to buy back (Nelson's Bible Dictionary, 2004). After Adam's debacle in the garden there was a lofty price set for mankind's redemption. The price was uncorrupted sinless blood, which was the only sacrifice that could satisfy or appease the demands of God's holiness. For this very reason when God came in the flesh it had to be an Immaculate Conception or virgin birth (read Matt. 1:20-24). He could not have been conceived by natural means of a husband and wife being sexually intimate and producing a baby.

Moreover, due to the fact that a baby's blood naturally comes from the father (that's why DNA test can be used to identify the father), and all normal children originate from human parents. Human beings naturally inherit a sinful nature passed down genetically from our forefather Adam. If Jesus had a biological father His blood would have been corrupted, which would have made it impossible for Him to become our redeemer.

The scriptures tell us: "Surely I was sinful at birth, sinful from the time my mother conceived me (Psalm 5:1, NIV). Thus, the only sacrifice that was suitable was Jesus the Christ not Mohammed, Buddha, Haile Selassie or Confucius (last I checked they all had biological fathers). "For you know that it was not with perishable things such as silver or gold that you were redeemed from the empty way of life handed down to you from your forefathers, but with the precious blood of Christ, a lamb without blemish or defect. He was chosen before the creation of the world, but was revealed in these last times for your sake (1 Pet. 1:18-20, NIV)."

Furthermore, some might ask, don't Christians sin too? Yes, we do and the scriptures are clear on that. However, though we struggle with sin and sometimes fall prey when we are not careful, we possess the innate power to resist and break the power of sinful habits off our lives and others. As Christians allow their minds to be renewed and grow in faith, our sins then become more of bad attitudes, sins of omission, motives, lack of faith, unbelief etc. and less sins of commission.

The word salvation is defined as: the act of saving or protecting from harm, risk, loss, or destruction; deliverance from the power and penalty of sin that results in redemption. Most of us might be more familiar with salvation producing deliverance from penalty of sin, i.e. hell (American Heritage Dictionary, 2004).

Albeit, salvation also sets us free from the power of sin, thus even though we will consistently struggle and be tempted, someone who is truly born again should not perpetually practice sin: "No one who is **born** of God will continue to **sin**, because God's seed remains in him; he cannot go on **sin**ning, because he has been **born** of God" (1 John 3:9, NIV).

Jesus announced His redemptive power by opening the scrolls the first scripture he quoted was this, which is the commencement of the redeeming process: "The Spirit of the Sovereign LORD is on me, because the LORD has anointed me to preach good news to the poor. He has sent me to bind up the broken-hearted, to proclaim freedom for the captives and release from darkness for the prisoners" (Isa. 61:1, NIV).

## Salvation
## "Born Again"

The *born again experience* is one of the most difficult concepts to understand when it comes to the salvation experience. Don't worry if you too feel a little perplexed about the subject, you are not alone. Nicodemus also struggled understanding it. Let us examine the dialogue: "Now there was a man of the Pharisees named Nicodemus, a member of the Jewish ruling council. He came to Jesus at night and said, Rabbi, we know you are a teacher who has come from God. For no one could perform the miraculous signs you are doing if God were not with him.

In reply Jesus declared, I tell you the truth, no one can see the kingdom of God unless he is born again. How can a man be born when he is old? Nicodemus asked. Surely he cannot enter a second time into his mother's womb to be born! Jesus answered, I tell you the truth, no one can enter the kingdom of God unless he is born of water and the Spirit" (John 3:1-5).

We can clearly understand that *born again* or the rebirth is not a physical, but rather metaphysical or spiritual experience. However, the proverbial question that needs to be understood is why there is a necessity for a rebirth experience? David in Psalm 51:5 let us know that we were conceived in sin and shaped in iniquity. When Adam and Eve sinned they inherited a sinful nature that became a fixed part of the human nature (refer back to Chapt. 2). Wherefore, everybody that would be born after Adam would automatically receive this corrupt nature at birth.

Please understand that we **all** come out of the womb as sinful children (due to Adam's sin). Example, have you ever wondered why you never have to teach a child how to lie, disobey, rebel, or do anything bad? That is because it comes natural, it's innately inclined. However, you do have to teach a child right, because even though they know right in their heart, they don't possess the power to regularly do it. They are however drawn to acting out the desires of their sinful nature.

Remember, our first parents didn't know wrong initially, they only knew good. If we review the historic and present day accounts we can see this sinful nature operating at its optimal degenerative levels, from cruel acts of slavery, human sacrifice, torture, child molestation, rape, incest, homosexuality, murder, etc.

These acts are from an immoral dysfunctional nature, which is far from God's righteous and holy nature. Many people will agree that people who engage in those gross acts are dysfunctional, but that's just the obvious.

Moreover, there are other acts that are less obvious and some are accepted in society. For example, lying, un-forgiveness, envy, gluttony, hatred, bitterness, resentment, gossip, pride, prejudices, uncontrolled anger, divisive motives, just to name a few. These are all characteristics that everyone can relate to and they are also traits along with the earlier list that's indicative of the sinful nature. Is it a wonder why the scriptures say that all have sinned? "Therefore, just as sin entered the world through one man, and death through sin, and in this way death came to all men, because **all sinned**" (Rom. 5:12).

Wherefore, it is explicitly concise that *all* are sinners, which means everyone is a born sinner no matter how morally good they think they are. We possess a morally degenerate sinful nature that is predisposed to committing sin and the nature is completely hostile to God, it is diabolic or from Satan. Paul wrote about the striving between the sinful nature and spirit in Romans chapter seven. The sinful nature always wants to have its way and it will never lead you to do anything that's right. It is a vicious battle for your will; the sinful nature wants to control your free will and anything that overpowers your choices is a vice and ultimately controls you.

Lastly, the proposed question many people have when it comes to salvation is how do I know that I'm saved? I don't want you to be troubled in your spirit and tormented in your mind regarding that question. Here are some of the ways you can be assured: Christ will be in your heart (Colossians 1:27), the inner witness of the Holy Spirit (Romans 8:16), answered prayer (John 14:14), experiencing real change in character (2 Corinthians 5:17), evidence of the fruit of the Spirit (Galatians 5:22), and possessing genuine love for people (1 John 3:14). Don't get discouraged if you don't experience everything at once, because all seeds take time to grow. However, there should be something growing in your garden out of the above list that corroborates the fact that you have been saved.

## Justification

Justification is a very powerful term when dealing with our salvation. For appropriate understanding of this term we must understand this is a legal term pronounced by God over those that are saved. "And those he predestined, he also called; those he called, he also justified; those he justified, he also glorified" (Rom. 8:30, NIV).

The opposite of condemnation is justification, so when God justified us He made the legal declaration that we were righteous. In other words justification is not something we can earn, neither is it something that we by ourselves deserved, but justification rests solely on the merits of God Himself.

Furthermore, justification is appropriated by grace through faith on our behalf, which means one cannot be justified without being born-again. "Therefore, since we have been justified through faith, we have peace with God through our Lord Jesus Christ, through whom we have gained access by faith into this grace in which we now stand" (Rom. 5:1-2, NIV). Justification then releases us from any future judgments of God.

Even though we deserved to be punished, God from his own righteousness exonerates us from our deserved punishment. Paul highlights the point in this scripture: "Therefore, there is now no condemnation for those who are in Christ Jesus" (Rom. 8:1, NIV).

## Regeneration

"Not by works of righteousness which we have done, but according to his mercy he saved us, by the washing of **regeneration**, and renewing of the Holy Ghost" (Titus 3:5, KJV).

Regeneration is defined as the process of spiritual rebirth or renewal. In order for mankind to reestablish a relationship with a Holy God, a dramatic and transformational change needed to transpire (Grudem, W. Systematic Theology). This is reverberated in the very words of Christ: "Marvel not that I said unto thee, ye **must** be born again" (John 3:7, KJV).

These words leave nothing to speculate, it is conveyed in black and white, "*you must be born again.*" The rebirth experience is then absolutely necessary and without it there can be no reconciliation between God and mankind.

Through the process of regeneration the spirit of mankind is quickened (made alive) by the Spirit of God, reconnecting that which was severed by Adam during the fall enabling the Holy Spirit to take up residence inside of mankind just like it was in the garden. Thus, the Holy Spirit then commences the process of sanctification, which I will discuss in great detail in the next chapter.

Regeneration is not just something that happens at conversion and then it is over; though our spirit is regenerated in the initial stages. Thus, regeneration is a process that is continuous throughout the life of a born-again Christian. It continues until we receive our glorified bodies, because our mind has to be reprogrammed to think differently than before. "Do not conform any longer to the pattern of this world, but be transformed by the renewing of your mind. Then you will be able to test and approve what God's will is—his good, pleasing and perfect will" (Rom. 12:2, NIV).

## Sanctification

I will probably lose many people here, but I must speak the truth in love. Too many of us have become over infatuated with the love of God. I understand that God is love! However, one of the most distinguishable attributes of God that may not be as commonly mentioned in churches is that God is Holy. And not only is he holy, but He places a requirement upon His people to also display that same characteristic. Peter carries this theme into the New Testament: "For it is written: Be holy, because I am holy (1 Peter 1:16)."

Unfortunately this term, like submission, may bring about much fear and intimidation upon many because we immediately start thinking about lofty, unreasonable and unattainable standards that we are unable to reach. How many people state that their new year's resolution is to attain another level of sanctification? You see this word is not something our carnal nature readily accepts or desires.

Too frequently, depending on your religious upbringing, this term unfortunately has been used in many mainline denominations to predominately control parishioner's outward appearance. Most people may be more familiar with the term holiness—however, holiness and sanctification can be used interchangeably, because they embody the exact definition. Definition: Hagiasmos {*Heb.* Strong's Greek/ Hebrew Definitions, 2004}, separation to God, the course of life befitting those separated the separation of the believer from evil things and evil ways.

Nevertheless, sanctification is not a word that any of us should have a need to fear—it is a term that is employed with great regularity throughout scripture. I want us to understand and appreciate the term, so I will break it down into three distinct phases that align with the scriptures: positional, progressive, and perfected.

First phase, positional holiness happens the moment you receive salvation, which ultimately changes your eternal position: "Do you not know that the wicked will not inherit the kingdom of God? Do not be deceived: Neither the sexually immoral nor idolaters nor adulterers nor male prostitutes nor homosexual offenders nor thieves nor the greedy nor drunkards nor slanderers nor swindlers will inherit the kingdom of God. And that is what **some of you were**. But you were washed, you were **sanctified**, you were justified in the name of the Lord Jesus Christ and by the Spirit of our God" (1 Corth. 6:9-11).

Notice this passage emphasizes what you used to do before you were sanctified. Sanctification connotes a change of position that results in a change in character and actions. Subsequently, all Christians are repositioned through the sanctification process as a new creature at conversion. "Therefore, if anyone is in Christ, he is a ***new creation***; the ***old has gone***, the new has come!" (2 Corth. 5:17, NIV).

Second phase, progressive holiness is centered on the journey of the Christian. No matter where we find ourselves in the process, we are in the process of sanctification as we strive towards maturity in the faith.

In addition, with the realization that we are walking through a process, which demands progress, we should not allow ourselves to become stagnated or complacent wherever we might find ourselves: "Press on toward the goal to win the prize for which God has called me heavenward in Christ Jesus" (Phil. 3:14, NIV). The more we grow in our relationship with God the more we progress in sanctification by understanding more of what God desires from us. God understood that we would fall and He has made provision for all of that, but the key is to understand that God is more concerned with the status of your heart than what you actually do.

The Bible already told us that we would fall, but we must learn from our falls and courageously try not to keep repeating the same mistakes: "For though a righteous man falls seven times, he rises again, but the wicked are brought down by calamity" (Prov. 24:16, NIV). Thus, continue to move forward in the process, even when you mess up. Don't allow the shame of sin to subject you to consternation.

Third phase, God is solely responsible for the first and the last phase of holiness. In 1 Corinthians15:42 Paul writes about the resurrection and how our mortal corrupted bodies will be exchanged for incorruptible ones. Yes, the finale or perfection is receiving a sanctified physical body fashioned like that of the resurrected body of Christ.

"Dear friends, now we are children of God, and what we will be has not yet been made known. But we know that when he appears, we shall be like him, for we shall see him as he is (1 John 3:2, NIV)."

Please understand that if you are truly born again, but like all of us you find your self with an assortment of short-comings and issues. However, don't get discouraged because of the sinful nature we inherited from the first Adam. Nevertheless, we are called to live a victorious life over sin. Remember, sin is not just committing some kind of ungodly act, but sin is also an attitude of the heart, and missing the mark. Yes, there are sins of commission and omission. However, the success of the last Adam ensured us that we can find forgiveness: "If we confess our sins, he is faithful and just and will forgive us our sins and purify us from all unrighteousness" (1 John 1:9, NIV). And because of the success of the last Adam mankind will once again repossess a body that knows no sin. Thus, perfection will be at the conclusion of the whole born again experience! Then God will make the cosmos return back to its original sinless uncorrupted state.

## Chapter 6

# Tribulation

Already I've dealt with many controversial subjects, but perhaps none greater than the doctrine of the rapture. .I will define the word rapture later: This long debated subject in Christendom has left the masses without clarity. The distinctive views include: pre-tribulational, mid-tribulational and post-tribulational. A myriad of cases have been presented for all the views. For those that might not be familiar with the tribulational terms here's what they mean:

1. Pre-Tribulation is the view that Christ will rapture the church, thus saving them from entering the tribulation.
2. Mid-Tribulational views the church being raptured at about the middle of the tribulation period.
3. Post-Tribulational views the church being not experiencing the rapture and being present throughout the whole tribulational period.

Albeit, before we can understand the rapture, we must first understand what the tribulation period is, what purpose does it serve? Keep in mind the terms are pertinent to appropriately understanding the eschatological order.

The Tribulational period is a futuristic seven-year period mentioned throughout scripture, where God's wrath and judgment are poured out on the entire world. The Bible refers to the tribulation in many different terms such as, The Day of the Lord (Isaiah. 2:12), Trouble or Tribulation (Deuteronomy. 4:30), The Great Tribulation (Matthew. 24:21), The Time or Day of Trouble (Daniel. 12:1), and Jacob's Trouble (Jeremiah. 30:7).

Throughout history all mankind have experienced catastrophes, devastations, trials, tribulation, pain and suffering. However, no matter how tragic these occurrences have been and continue to be—there's nothing that has happened throughout earth's history that will be remotely able to compare to the tribulation period. Here are a few scriptures that affirm that astounding point:

"And at that time shall Michael stand up, the great prince which stands for the children of thy people: and there shall be a time of trouble, such as never was since there was a nation even to that same time: and at that time thy people shall be delivered, every one that shall be found written in the book" (Dan. 12:1, KJV).

"How awful that day will be! None will be like it. It will be a time of trouble for Jacob, but he will be saved out of it "(Jerm. 30:7, KJV).

"For then shall be great tribulation, such as was not since the beginning of the world to this time, no, nor ever shall be" (Matt. 24:21, KJV).

"Now, brothers, about times and dates we do not need to write to you, for you know very well that the day of the Lord will come like a thief in the night. While people are saying, Peace and safety, destruction will come on them suddenly, as labor pains on a pregnant woman, and they will not escape" (1 Thes. 5:1-2, NIV)

The essence of the tribulation period is a time of testing; it is a time of purging and purifying, a time of destruction, vengeance, and woe that will fall upon the disobedient inhabitants of the earth the tribulation is for those who for one reason or the other would not make Jesus Christ their Lord and Savior. The scripture labels those people disobedient, because they neglect the only way of escape from eminent destruction. "Let no one deceive you with empty words, for because of such things God's wrath comes on those who are disobedient" (Eph. 5:6, NIV).

The tribulation is also called Jacob's trouble (Jerm. 30:7) because God will deal with Israel or the Jews. God's attention will be focused on purifying Israel and once again the gospel will be predominantly preached by the Jews (just like it was at the conception of the church). Paul wrote about the olive tree and how we the Gentiles were grafted in (Rom. 11), but the Jews make up the natural branches. God's plan for salvation was inclusive for both Jews and Gentiles alike, but the Jews were temporally put aside because of their unbelief. However, God will restore His natural branch and all Israel will be saved when the Gentile period has ended. "I do not want you to be ignorant of this mystery, brothers, so that you may not be conceited: Israel has experienced a hardening in part until the full number of the Gentiles has come in. And so all Israel will be saved, as it is written: The deliverer will come from Zion; he will turn godlessness away from Jacob. And this is my covenant with them when I take away their sins" (Rom. 11:25-27, NIV.)

Some might be wondering, does that mean that no more gentiles will be saved during the tribulation? That is a great question. To make it simple, even though we currently live in the era of the gentiles, Jewish people are still being saved everyday though it is not considered the time of the Jews. The time of the gentile's means that God's focused plan of salvation is on the gentiles predominantly. This will be reversed during the time of Jacob's trouble. Gentiles will still be saved, but God's redemptive plan will then be mainly about the Jews.

## Heirs of Salvation

Now that we understand what the tribulational period is and its purpose the question we must ask ourselves, is it something God will take us through? Let's examine a few scriptures to see if that can be corroborated by the Word: "For God hath not appointed us to wrath, but to obtain salvation by our Lord Jesus Christ, Who died for us, that, whether we wake or sleep, we should live together with him"(1 Thes. 5:9-10, KJV).

"Since we have now been justified by his blood, how much more shall we be saved from God's **wrath** through him!" (Rom. 5:9, NIV). "Since you have kept my command to endure patiently, I will also keep you from the hour of trial that is going to come upon the whole world to test those who live on the earth" (Rev. 3:10, NIV).

According to the facts presented, the tribulation is a special time of the pouring out of God's wrath and indignation, and that point I have more than corroborated with the Bible. The scripture distinctively tells us that born-again saints are not appointed or will be subject to God's wrath. The deliberation of God is clear concerning His church; we will go through trials, storms, and tribulations. However, we will be delivered from out of the Great Tribulation because salvation worked out deliverance for those that received it.

## The word Rapture

One of the issues that have spawned much confusion pertaining to the understanding of timing of the rapture is the misappropriation of two terms: eschatology and ecclesiology. Eschatology is a theological term dealing with the study of end-time events. Meanwhile, ecclesiology theologically signifies the study of the nature of the church.

One of the keys to understanding the proper context of when the rapture will take place is to know that even though rapture is an end-time event, it is more of a matter of ecclesiology because it is a dynamic concerning the church.

This understanding will allow us to be released from the handcuffs of our minds trying to make something fit in a place not intended for it. There are certain distinctive benefits that were exclusive to the church alone. The nature of the church can be easily overlooked even by theologians and students of Bible prophecy.

In addition, throughout church history there have been many debates in regards not only to this particular subject, but about the word itself. The reason being you will not find this specific word in any of the sixty–six books in your Bible. Here's what the word means: r*apture-* "the experience, anticipated by some fundamentalist Christians, of meeting Christ midway in the air upon his return to earth" (dictionary.com).

The word rapture finds its scriptural context in the following text: "For the Lord himself will come down from heaven, with a loud command, with the voice of the archangel and with the trumpet call of God, and the dead in Christ will rise first. After that, we who are still alive and are left will be **caught up** together with them in the clouds to meet the Lord in the air" (1 Thess. 4:16-17, KJV).

As noted earlier the scripture doesn't utilize the actual word (rapture); however the term rapture comes from the Greek word Harpozô, which connotates the word **snatching up**. Thus, its usage is appropriately used in its context. There are many other terms that we comfortable utilize and that are not written in the Bible for example, Millennium, but we accept it because it adequately conveys the 1000 year reign of Christ on the earth. Thus, employing the word rapture to articulate an event in scripture should not be the substratum to any debate concerning this subject. Now that we have graciously dealt with verbiage let's move forward.

Chapter 7

# The Bride

For many of us that have been in church long enough we understand that the bride of Christ speaks of the ecclesia (called out ones) or those that are born again within the Christian church. One of the worst things that ever happened to the church was the separation from its Jewish brothers. I said that because whether we like it or not Jesus was

Jewish by nationality and birth. The Bible was written by mostly Jews to a predominant Jewish audience.

Therefore, there are certain concepts and idioms that are native to the Jews that we might not readily understand as Westerners or non-Jewish people. We can all grasp the understanding that there are certain traditions that are inclusive to different cultures.. The Bible by no means eludes this very principle, so why do we read or study the scriptures with our own modern non-Jewish mindset? Never taking the time to study Jewish history or culture, inevitably leads to misinterpreting the scriptures. It is simply our lens we use does not allow us to see clearly, it is like trying to use 3-D glasses on an old black and white television (it doesn't work).

Subsequently, we do have a profusion of denominations within Christendom, many variances in doctrinal beliefs, a nebulous understanding of the scripture; and we sometimes feel the Bible is too archaic and irrelevant for today's world. It is just an old book full of good stories.

However, if we just took the time to delve into some Jewish cultural history we can assume the proper lenses to rightly divide the word of truth and exegete the scriptures accurately. Is it then any wonder why there's so many different views on the rapture? I respect all views pertaining to this event, but if it is truth we are after then let us scrutinize the facts and see what view makes more sense.

Moreover, one thing we can appreciate is Jesus never used any idle or vain words. In other words, everything He spoke articulated some type of meaning to his audience. The term bride can't be taken lightly, it encapsulates significant meaning. The bride of Christ is not only a term but it represents a model for the rapture below are some scriptures written about the bride: "I hope you will put up with a little of my foolishness; but you are already doing that. I am jealous for you with a godly jealousy. I promised you to one husband, to Christ, so that I might present you as a pure virgin to him" (2 Corth 11:1-2, NIV).

"Husbands, love your wives, just as Christ loved the church and gave himself up for her to make her holy, cleansing her by the washing with water through the word, and to present her to himself as a radiant church, without stain or wrinkle or any other blemish, but holy and blameless. In this same way, husbands ought to love their wives as their own bodies. He who loves his wife loves himself. After all, no one ever hated his own body, but he feeds and cares for it, just as Christ does the church— for we are members of his body. For this reason a man will leave his father and mother and be united to his wife, and the two will become one flesh. This is a profound mystery—but I am talking about Christ and the church" (Ephs. 5:25-32, NIV).

Notice, in the above scripture how Paul starts off talking about husbands and wives and then paralleled that relationship to Christ and the church. Thus, the Bible makes it vividly clear that we are the bride of Christ, which should prompt us to desire to know what it might mean to us today.

## Ancient Jewish Weddings

Ancient Jewish wedding were completely different from the traditional weddings of the modern world. First, the father of the groom would choose his son's bride; we see an example of this in Genesis 24. The Father also chose His Son's bride: "According as he hath chosen us in him before the foundation of the world, that we should be holy and without blame before him in love: Having predestinated us unto the adoption of children by Jesus Christ to himself, according to the good pleasure of his will, To the praise of the glory of his grace, wherein he hath made us accepted in the beloved" (Eph. 1:4-6, KJV).

Second, the father of the bride would then establish a price (mohair), which we also can see in Genesis 24. There was of course a hefty price to pay for us: "Forasmuch as ye know that ye were not redeemed with corruptible things, as silver and gold, from your vain conversation received by tradition from your fathers; But with the precious blood of Christ, as of a lamb without blemish and without spot" (1 Pet. 1:18-19, KJV).

Third, once the agreement was made, a contract was drawn up which listed the responsibilities of each party, along with the agreed upon price to be paid. The process was usually consummated by the drinking of wine from a shared cup. (Does this sound familiar?). The actual marriage ceremony has not yet taken place; however the process resulted in a legal binding marriage, thus completing the "betrothal" stage. We can find an excellent example of this in Matthew 1:18-24. Mary was betrothed to Joseph, but we know that they had yet to have any type of sexual intimacy. Nevertheless, she was still considered Joseph's wife and if he wanted to divorce her, he had to go through the normal divorce proceedings of his day.

Someone might be wondering when did Jesus accomplish this task? When did we participate in this process and what covenant was established? Have you ever participated in a Eucharist or Communion service? Have you ever read the New Covenant or New Testament? "While they were eating, Jesus took bread, gave thanks and broke it, and gave it to his disciples, saying, Take and eat; this is my body. Then he took the cup, gave thanks and offered it to them, saying, Drink from it, all of you. This is my blood of the covenant, which is poured out for many for the forgiveness of sins" (Matt 26:26-28, NIV).

Fourth, the groom would now leave his bride and go back to his father's house to prepare a place for her. Ironically this is the same exact promise Jesus made: "In my Father's house are many rooms; if it were not so, I would have told you. I am going there to prepare a place for you. And if I go and prepare a place for you, I will come back and take you to be with me that you also may be where I am" (John 14:2-3, NIV).

Fifth, it then becomes necessary for the bride to prepare, be faithful, and anticipate her groom's return. The groom would surprisingly come back (like a thief) for his bride with accompanied with celebration with shouting and blowing of the shofar or trumpets. We can find this very event in the following scripture:

"For the Lord himself will come down from heaven, with a loud command, with the voice of the archangel and with the trumpet call of God, and the dead in Christ will rise first. After that, we who are still alive and are left will be caught up together with them in the clouds to meet the Lord in the air" (1 Thes. 4:16-17, NIV).

Lastly, if you think the previous points have been intriguing, then you will be fascinated by this one. The groom would then take his bride back to his father's house for a ceremony—immediately following the ceremony (which was only for a few invited guests) the bride and groom would have a seven day feast. Upon the time of the feast they entered into the wedding chamber (huppah) where the marriage would be finally consummated.

Is it by coincidence that the seven days in the bridal chamber correspond with the seven year tribulational period? Some might be saying well seven days and the years don't correlate. Sure it does when you are dealing with God's watch: "But do not forget this one thing, dear friends: With the Lord a day is like a thousand years, and a thousand years are like a day" (1 Pet. 3:8, NIV).

The special feast is written in the scripture, some of you will better know it as the marriage supper: "And he saith unto me, Write, Blessed are they which are called unto the marriage supper of the Lamb. And he saith unto me, these are the true sayings of God" (Rev. 19:9, KJV). "Come, my people, enter thou into thy chambers, and shut thy doors about thee: hide thyself as it were for a little moment, until the indignation be overpast. For, behold the LORD cometh out of his place to punish the inhabitants of the earth for their iniquity: the earth also shall disclose her blood, and shall no more cover her slain (Isa. 26:20-21, KJV).

## Conclusion

I, for one, believe it proposes great difficulty to understand something without knowing the origin. Thus, we have dealt with a diversified set of subjects in detail in order to answer the one proposed question: Saved from What? If I've proficiently done my job in presenting the facts while sifting through the scriptures, then we should know by now that salvation worked great deliverance for us in many arenas and facets. We are saved from sin, death and destruction, the great tribulation, and an eternity of separation from God. Jesus successfully reacquired our rights back from the enemy of our souls by paying the king's ransom with His one-hundred percent precious royal blood.

Moreover, I find it ironic that Jesus' first miracle was performed at a wedding (where He turned water into wine as stated in John 2:9) and it all ends in a wedding feast. This point demonstrates that God is a God who is solely motivated by love! The relationship that I see between God and the church is one of romance. Yes, my friend, God is quite romantic to the point that He laid out a contingency plan of love, possessing the foreknowledge that Adam would fail. "For God so loved the world that he gave his only begotten son that whosoever believe in him should not perish, but have everlasting life" (John 3:16).

Therefore, let us stop taking the privilege that's been afforded to us for granted. It cost Jesus his life and blood to reconcile us back from the curse of the sin and death. He interposed himself and took our place on that cross, so we can lay hold on eternal life. However, if you don't take advantage of what God did and refuse to accept His free gift it will cost you for all eternity. Please stop rolling the dice on forever, this is your day and appointed time.

The scriptures tell us that the only two things needed for us to be saved are faith in Jesus and confession from our mouths: "That if you <u>confess</u> with your mouth, Jesus is Lord, and <u>believe</u> in your heart that God raised him from the dead, you will be <u>saved</u>" (Rom. 10:9, NIV). Repeat after me: "Father forgive me of my sins. I rededicate myself to you today and I accept Jesus Christ as my personal Lord and Savior. Come into my heart, Lord, and change me into a new person. Amen."

If you prayed that prayer and meant it, then the angels and I are rejoicing over your born-again soul—I would officially like to welcome you to the Faith! It's not a perfect world filled with perfect people, but we all serve the one who is perfect in all His ways. Stay tuned for my next book the sequel, Saved for What? Now that you are saved, what does God want you to do with the rest of your life?

## Topical Study Guide

**Salvation**...................... Romans 8:16; Colossians 1:27; Galatians. 5:22; 2 Corth. 5:17; John 14:14, 3:1-5, 3:16; 1 John 3:14

**Born Again**.................... Romans 5:12, 7; John 3:1-5

**Justification**.................. Romans 8:30, 5:12, 8:1

**Regeneration**................... Titus 3:5; John 3:7; Romans 12:2

**Sanctification**................ 1 Peter 1:16; Philippians. 3; 14; John 3:2; 1 John 1:9; 1 Corinthians 6:9-11, 15:42; 2 Corinthians 5:17

**Tribulation**............... Isaiah 2:12; Deuteronomy 4:30; Jer. 30:7; Daniel 12:1; Matthew 24:21; Romans 5:9, 11; Ephesians 5:6; Revelation 3:10; 1 Thessalonians 5:1-2

**Rapture**....................... 1 Thessalonians 4:16-17; 2 Corinthians 11:1-2; 1 Peter 1:18-19; Ephesians 5:25-32; John 14:2-3; Isaiah 26:20-21

# Bibliography

Grudem, W. (2000). An *Introduction to Biblical Doctrine Systematic Theology:* Grand Rapids, Michigan: Zondervan

Grenz, G. (2000). *Theology for the Community of God:* Grand Rapids, Michigan: Broadman & Holman

Landman, I. (1948) *The Universal Jewish Encyclopedia*: New York: Universal Jewish Encyclopedia Co., Inc.

Morris M. H., (1981) *The Bible Has the Answer:* Ada, MI: Baker Publishing Group

Strong's Greek/Hebrew Definitions (2004). PC Study Bible (Version 4.2B) [Computer Software] Seattle, WA: Bible Soft

New Ungler's Bible Dictionary (2004). PC Study Bible (Version 4.2B) [Computer Software] Seattle, WA: Bible Soft

Nelson's Bible Dictionary (2004). PC Study Bible (Version 4.2B) [Computer Software] Seattle, WA: Bible Soft

American Heritage Dictionary (2004). PC Study Bible (Version 4.2B) [Computer Software] Seattle, WA: Bible Soft

Mace R. D., *Hebrew Marriage*, Philosophical Library, New York, 1953, p.167.

http://www.biblegateway.com

http://dictionary.com

www.ingramcontent.com/pod-product-compliance
Lightning Source LLC
LaVergne TN
LVHW091151051225
827140LV00008B/151
* 9 7 8 1 6 0 9 5 7 8 3 6 7 *